Slow Wreckage

Slow Wreckage

poems

Barbara Crooker

GRAYSON BOOKS
West Hartford, Connecticut
graysonbooks.com

"…this far down
the path to dust"
Christopher Buckley, "Drought"

"I'm going down slow"
St. Louis Jimmy Oden, "Going Down Slow"

For Richard, da cuore

Contents

VI

Then

The past is never dead. It's not even past.
—*William Faulkner*

Oak leaves stamped against a chicory sky
swirled with clouds, like a marble I once had
and lost. It's probably still there, caught in a dry
puddle, a tree root, or one of those cracked

pavements of childhood that we walked
on going to school. We roamed the neighborhood
in feral packs, marked up the curb with chalk:
hopscotch, marbles, kickball, only going in for food

or band-aids. No sunscreen, helmets, fancy bikes.
Once, we rode to the creek to swim, dead deer
resting in the shallows. We didn't think alike:
was it safe to swim, or not? I can still hear

my mother calling my name as darkness fell
and fireflies sent messages that only they could spell.

On Teaching Poetry Classes in My Old Elementary School in Honor of Its 100th Anniversary

Yes, I know my mother isn't there, as I walk up and down
Main Street; she's moved to a different zip code, the one
with no returns. When I was twenty, I worked for the summer
here at 12524, sorting mail in the morning, taking down
the flag at night. If you were to look at Main Street, facing east,
you'd see not much has changed since the 1900's, except
there's no trolley now, and the street is paved. But I'm still hoping
to see her, maybe in Stern's department store, the one that carried
summer cardigans. Or at the Busy Bee having a milk shake, frothy
in the glass, the rest of it waiting in a cold aluminum tumbler
on the side. I'm looking for her friend Winnie, whose mind left
long before her body failed; she might be buying a card
in Rabbit's Pharmacy. Or for Marian, Ginger's mother; she might
be picking up dinner at Karl Ehmer meats or the Bogardus
General Store. I'm looking for the deep shade of old trees, moss
on the sidewalks, maple wings stuck on the noses of boys ...
Here is the Dutch Reformed church that served as a jail
in the Revolution. Here's the bend in the creek
where we used to go swimming, the railroad tracks we crossed
in winter to the frozen pond beyond. Here is the street
where we went sledding; this is childhood's end. But
my mother's not there, nor her friends, nor mine. All the shops
have changed hands, been renamed. Only the mountains remain,
row after row of every shade of green; women taking their ease
and resting, after their long day's work is finally done.

Diorama

A shoe box set on its side.
The knotty pine paneling brown.
A small nuclear family
in early American chairs.
Macaroni and cheese in the oven,
the crust thickening on a loaf
of banana bread. The den
an altar to the black & white TV.
There's a fireplace in the living room,
but no smoke in the chimney, and no one
listens to the hi-fi, where records,
shiny black platters, once spun, music
threading from the scratchy needle.
Mother stands by the stove, waiting
to serve. Father has tamped down
his anger for the night. The children
are quiet, waiting for the future.

Mussels

My parents rented a small house by the sea;
it was the fifties, and this was a stretch for them.
It wasn't on the ocean, but several blocks inland,
and not the Atlantic itself, but Long Island Sound.
A brackish stream sullenly nudged nearby;
the smell of plough mud enough to bring me back.
My immigrant grandmother came each year;
she knew the art of making do, led us in the hunt
for steamer clams (look for squirts or holes in the sand),
scuttling crabs, and mussels, those hard blue nuggets
we plucked from rocks at low tide. Strangers
gathered around us, wondered what we were doing.
Food came from the supermarket, a new abundance
after the war, not the damp sand. *What on earth will you
do with them, then?* they asked, not knowing how
they would transform in the kettle's steam into something
sweet and delicious, glistening with olive oil, nuggets
of garlic, a splash of wine, making the bed of linguine
sing. Our family wasn't an easy one—my father's anger
always on the back burner, my mother and grandmother
in conflict in the kitchen—but here, we earned our dinner
foraging together. We twirled our forks in the tangled
strands, and dug in.

Obsolescence

My mother's silver sifter:
turn the handle,
start the tumbler:

a spill of pollen. And
an anachronism in the age
of take-out and name brands

labeled homemade.
Who now cuts lard
into flour and salt with the blade

of a pastry knife? Hard
to believe in the crimp
between thumb and fore-

finger, fluting the rim.
Who kneads bread dough
then waits for yeast to begin

its miracle, growing
to double in size?
Who rescues potatoes,

carrots, onions, sighing
in the crisper, turns them into
soup or stew? Praise

those who turn scraps to new
quilts, hook wool into rugs,
crochet unraveled blue

yarn into blankets that hug
the bony shoulders of the homeless,
the discarded, the sidewalk's dregs.

Pentimento

In the lost rooms of my childhood,
cinnamon and nutmeg float in the air,
sprinkle the kitchen with notes of brown,
and my mother rolls out leftover pie crust
into an irregular circle, which she brushes
with butter, kisses with sugar and spice.
Scrolls it into a fat cylinder, slices it
into rounds. She slides the silver tray
into the oven, and a bit of heaven
drifts into my teenage bedroom,
where angst still lingers. Later, she'll use
my grandmother's recipe to simmer sauce,
molten red lava, redolent tones of oregano,
basil, thyme. Time cannot run backwards,
no matter how hard we try. No matter
how much we miss what isn't there: the drag
from her cigarette, the jangle of ice cubes,
the juniper, the gin.

Car Hop

I was twenty, my last summer working at Patty's Charcoal Drive-In, senior year in college coming up, and what on earth was I going to do next? I made seventy-five cents an hour, plus tips. All those shiny quarters. Some went down the throat of the jukebox—*96 Tears, What Becomes of the Brokenhearted, Reach Out / I'll Be There*. Most of them went to pay for my education, something my grandchildren will never understand, but still possible in the late sixties. What my father, child of immigrants, didn't understand was why I didn't get a job after high school—I was a girl, after all, who did I think I was? Who cared if I was second in my class, honors and advance placements, aced my Regents exams? At least I didn't have to worry about the jungles of southeast Asia, like the boys in my class. But what was I going to do with this degree in English Literature and Art History? I was tired of waiting on cars full of boys going nowhere, catching that *Last Train to Clarksville*. The Stones were singing *Paint it Black*, and *California Dreamin'* seemed as impossible as going to the moon. I was terrified that my father was right, and some endless office job was on the horizon: alphabetizing, filing; touch typing and steno skills, was that all I was good for? This empty parking lot, burger wrappers rattling the edges in the sticky August wind. The world already shifting, but none of us knew it yet.

Queens

We are all just walking each other home.
—Ram Dass

I hadn't taken the subway in fifty years, not since
I was an undergraduate, and I was nervous.

Back then, it was hard to navigate, as graffiti and peace
signs covered up the maps. But a friend from Queens

wanted to meet for lunch, so I took a deep breath
and set out, clutching the email she'd sent with directions.

Of course, now the maps are electronic, not readily
broken, and easy to read. But her station was confusing,

a maze of underground passages, and she'd warned me
I'd have to walk some distance if I went up the wrong

stairs. So I stood there, trying to align her text, match
her words to the nearby stores. An elderly East Asian

woman asked, *You lost?* She snatched the papers
from my hand. *Okay. Follow me.* Wielding her cane

like a weapon, she pushed pedestrians out of the way,
held it up like a banner as we crossed against the light.

She pointed out the "good" fruit stands, wagged her finger
at the "bad" ones, ignored the storefronts with elaborate

gold jewelry. She was my Italian grandmother, in a different skin.
When we reached my destination, she gave me back my papers.

Turn here. Friend lives there. And when I turned to thank her, she was gone. Above, in the stunted city trees: the wind through

the leaves, the sound of rustling wings.

Mirror

Who *is* this woman in my mirror,
the one who looks like she's been
worked on by Rembrandt or Dürer?
Why are there mail sacks sagging under
her chin? Wasn't it just last week
I was doing my hair on rollers
the size of orange juice cans?
Why is my scalp, pink as an eraser,
showing through? What happened
to my snappy ponytail that switched
and danced when I cheered? I still feel fresh
as the first day of school, new plaid skirt,
box of sharpened crayons, pencils that no one
has written with yet. Why is this young man
from down the street shoveling my driveway?
Doesn't he know my shoulders have lifted
great burdens? Can't he see I've already hefted
huge shovelfuls of sorrows and stars?

American Plane Tree

The sycamores are shedding again,
the lawn littered with their mottled bark:
mourning dove gray, butternut, ash.
This is their yearly strip to the bones,
the trunk cool and smooth to the touch.
But first, it's scabrous, thin strips peeling
and hanging, like spent skin after a bad
sunburn. I want to scale the tree
like a lumberjack, rip off the rest. Which,
of course, I can't; yet again a reminder
how flawed, this one life. A friend
I saw recently suddenly died. This country,
a runaway train. Foxes in the henhouses.
Weather askew: fires incinerate the west,
flash floods drown the east. The sycamore
doesn't care. Each year, another ring.
An inch of girth. An applause of leaves.
And then the great
letting go.

On a Late Birthday

No one wants to hear about it,
the body's slow wreckage:
skin cracking like porcelain
left in the kiln too long,
words that recede mid-sentence
like the slow-ebbing tide.
A string of minor infirmities
I tell like a rosary: the need
for more breath going up hills;
the clarity of events from ten years ago,
while yesterday is cloudy weather.
Sleep that fails to come, the digital clock
at 3 am. Knees on the stairs, refusing
to hinge. Spots on the hand that mimic
the small toad I found sunk in mud
in a corner of the vegetable garden last spring.

II

Seventieth Birthday

That evening, I sat at a table
with a linen cloth, elegant cocktail
of lemon vodka, champagne, elder-
flower liqueur, stars in my ears.
Across from me, the man I still
love, his silver hair glinting
in the dim half-light. I'm thinking
of Jane Kenyon, and how this could be
otherwise. But it's not. I know later
there'll be an empty chair. A cold bed.
A life halved. But right now, I have
everything I need: the sun coming up
tomorrow morning, the clouds, pink frosting
spreading all the way to the horizon.

Aphorisms at Seventy

Now "when" becomes "if."

The horizon starts to lower.

You realize you have a sell-by date.

And the deer are always going to win
    the battle of the garden.

You will never become reconciled
    to losing friends.

You are not going to lose the weight
    from that last baby.

Or finish your reading list.

Still, red wine goes with everything.

There is always chocolate.

Spring never gets old.

You don't need a partner to dance.

I Want to Write a Poem to Celebrate

the body, its mystery as it ages,
the scars, the lines, the silver threads
unwinding. I no longer care about air-brushed
celebrities in glossy magazines. I want
to celebrate weak ankles courtesy of afternoons
chasing a puck on a frozen pond. Thighs,
more Venus of Willendorf than Kate Moss
or Twiggy. Upper arms that wobble like Jello
no matter how many reps I do at the gym. Belly
that stretched big as a watermelon, then spit out
(how did that happen?) sweet pink babies.
Breasts that fed them, rivers of thin blue milk.
I've made the turn onto the unpaved road,
where fat yellow leaves hang overhead. Things
don't get better from here. But over there,
in the clearing, beyond the fields of goldenrod,
New England asters, pearly everlasting,
they're waiting: the friends who've gone before,
my parents, grandparents, lost baby. They've
set up a picnic: checked tablecloth, sourdough
bread, French cheeses, green grapes, red wine.
The air is sweet with fermentation and birdsong.
The sun slants in from the west and, like Midas,
paints everything gold.

Who Do You Carry?

Still here I carry my old delicious burdens.
—Walt Whitman, "Song of the Open Road"

For years, I carried my mother, though
she grew lighter and lighter, letting go
of her possessions with every move,
until, at the end, there were only her clothes,
left to be bagged for Goodwill. Untethered
by her oxygen tank, she floated away—
Today I carry my son, whose body's an adult,
but whose mind is a small child's.
My burden—his future when I am gone—
is heavy, the social safety net ripped,
holes big enough to sail a boat through.
On city streets, the homeless unfurl
their sleeping bags like hungry tongues.
The "lucky ones" have tents in a vacant lot.
How have we come to this, Walt Whitman?
It's the Twenty-First century, in America.
Can you still hear us singing?

Weight Training

and how can you train
the body to be the body?
—Carrie Addington, "Waist Training"

How can I train this body,
with its baggage, the freight
load of dinners in France, plates
gleaming with sauce and cream,
sauté pans sizzling, a glass of rosé
at the start of the meal that's raised
to the setting sun? Breakfast: an array
of croissants in a basket, display
of *confitures*, especially *les fraises
des bois*, wild strawberries. Cushioned
in a chair, I'm sedentary: at my keyboard
writing essays or reading a roman à clef.
The days when I ran before dawn, gone.
Praise be to my left knee; the right one says
mercy going down stairs. The pain in places
I never knew existed. Ahead, there's a station
and I'm slowly chugging towards it.
No weight training at the gym
or miles on the exercycle can stay this decline.
In the passenger car, a conductor sways,
pushing his clicker, punching tickets: sprays
of confetti, little o's litter the aisles, ricochet.

Treadmill

after "We Real Cool" by Gwendolyn Brooks

We lift weights. We
feel great. We

do yoga. We
eat granola. We

ride bikes. We
take hikes. We

sip green tea. We
do Pilates. We

swim laps. Don't
take naps. We

run miles. We
dress in style. We're

the Baby Boom. We
die soon.

Degenerative Disc Disorder

Three weeks in pain, on a scale of one to ten, a twelve,
and no sleep to speak of, just what I can snatch
sitting upright in a chair, ice pack behind my back,
taking the best pharmaceuticals insurance can provide,
which don't bring it down, not even a notch.

And what I miss most of all isn't sleep, no,
it's the bedding—the rose flannel sheets,
the quilt we bought from the Mennonites
that's fallen into threads—we can't replace
it because so much love happened under its log
cabin blocks—the pillow that molds to my body
like an extra arm, one with billowing flesh—
I miss being *horizontal*, feeling my bones suspend,
floating in night's dark pond, anchored
to your familiar body, its steady warmth,
the way you let me slip my icy feet
under your thighs. Not sex; I can't imagine sex—
that's something from another country, far away.

No, I am marooned, downstairs, on an island
of pain, in a night that won't end, waiting
for a day that promises no better. My spine
is disintegrating, falling in pieces, hooks
and barbs that cause the muscles to spasm
and clench. And there they sit, those harpies,
jabbing their cruel little feet on a nerve.
While upstairs, the sleepers nestle deeper
in their covers, their breaths rising,
yeast in the sweet bread of morning.

Acupuncture

She sticks the needles in,
gives them a little twist,
tries to engage the nerve,
to release the blocked chi,
to let the stopped-
up energy run
like a river.
She sticks in another silver
needle, turns it once,
and my arm jumps
like a frog's in 10th grade
Biology class. *Balance in all things,*
Dr. Ming says, *will give you*
good health and a long life.
She pushes the next needle deeper.
Cold/Hot, Dark/Light, Moon/Sun,
all the opposites struggle
to line up inside me.
Yin and Yang,
the wax and the flame.
Wood, earth, fire, water
compete for attention.
She says *relax, lie still,*
this pain is not real,
let go of unhealthy influences.
My back bristles, a human porcupine.
I want my fingers to return:
the mute pinky I never appreciated,
the numb ring finger
that used to wear my wedding band.
But I must be blocked
in every meridian.

Dr. Ming says *practice patience.*
Open your heart
like a many-petalled lotus.
Hope is the golden spine of the sun.

After Rotator Cuff Surgery

And if your right hand causes you to sin, cut it off and throw it away; it is better to lose one of your members than that your whole body go into hell.
—Matthew 5:30

The weather of my shoulder:
a sunset of bruises
occluding the skin, forming
storm clouds, a formidable line
of squalls. Royal purple.
Blue black. My arm, my hockey-
playing right wing, hangs limply
at my side, a dumb sausage,
or swings at right angles
in its canvas sling.
The starboard side
has listed to port.

I cannot:
line my eyes with carbon brown,
buckle my sandals, or clasp
my watch. Can't drive stick
shift, cut up steak, dead
head roses, swipe the cool
ball of deodorant under
my arms. Lift a kettle
of water to boil for sweet corn.
I'm a wreck on the recto side.
But at least I've never voted
for a right-winger, and I do
know my right hand from my left,
my hat from my glove.

I go back to cataloguing
bruises: swirls of magenta
and burgundy blooming
into hideous roses.
I sink back in the recliner,
hugging the ice bag, high
on Percocet, rocking
in the waters
of the sweet black night.

After Oral Surgery,

I start to forget how much I like to eat:
baguettes shattering into splinters;
salted popcorn, its kernels lethal
now; oatmeal cookies, crumbs

that infiltrate the gaping crater.
Now I'm in the land of bland, living
on creamed soups, mashed potatoes,
coddled eggs .... Anything with cayenne,

Tabasco, jalapeños would electrify
these throbbing open sockets ...
Even though I'm almost a vegetarian,
I start to dream about steak, charbroiled,

sputtering and hissing, blood pooling
on the plate. I might as well imagine
eating my pillow. Night seems endless,
stomach mumbling, talking out loud.

I envy those models in commercials
whose encounters with food
border on the pornographic.
They never chew or swallow,

but oh, what ecstasies of foreplay.
Meanwhile, my poor gums thrum
with pain. What I wouldn't give for one
brief tryst with a hot slice of buttered toast ....

III

U Pick

Hot July morning, sun a burner left on high. Raspberries,
beveled treasures; sour pie cherries, ruby globes, filling
the cardboard picking box. I'm by myself, listening to the chatter
of my neighbors in adjoining rows. Some of us are up on ladders;
some are down in the brambles and briars. We all think we're
in high heaven, after the long winter, late cold spring. If this
were a protest march, would a few be carrying opposite signs,
shouting invectives? Maybe so, but we're here in this small
orchard, sharing recipes, tips on preserves, how to make
a good pie. We cradle our baskets as if they contain unruly jewels.
And then we go our separate ways, licked by the thick tongue
of the sun, to bring some sweetness to our families,
blinking our blind eyes in the multilingual light.

And It's Hard

It's April, and a hard rain is falling,
   just as Bob Dylan told us it would,
and every day, the news on the radio
   is worse. Well-greased gobs of lies coming
out of Washington, cabinet-level appointments
   of people least qualified for the job,
and nobody wants to talk about climate change,
   although we should all be terrified. Bob warned
you've got to serve somebody, and look, there's
   Satan at the head of the line, tray in hand,
hoping for a second helping of duplicity and greed,
   the blue-plate special. Dana Carvey used to smirk,
isn't that special in the voice of The Church Lady,
   but it isn't any more. *More more more* is
the motto of the day for CEOs and billionaires—

   I've been trying to cut down, scale back,
skip lunch. But then comes Christmas, which
   looks like an elf threw up in your house according
to my son-in-law—twenty kinds of cookies,
   the Holy Trinity of sugar, butter, and eggs—
enough tinsel, glitter, and tiny white lights to be seen
   from a satellite. What this has to do with the birth
of a baby in a barn, I'm not quite sure. But I know
   something is falling, and I've got to keep hoping it's scales
from the hardened hearts of the powerful, the way vinegar
   removes lime from a tea kettle, and that somehow, despite
the fix, the darkening odds, a little light will shine.

Love in These Dangerous Times

Sitting across from you, glass
of wine in hand, I'm warmed by
the little gas fire, secure as I think
about the cave we'll make when
we go upstairs: flannel sheets,
duvet of goose down. Tomorrow,
we will go out again in the dangerous
world, wearing face masks and gloves,
in search of produce and toilet paper,
trying to make our supplies stretch.
When we return, we'll feel like heroes
in a quest saga, safely home. But nothing
and nowhere is safe, my love. So hold me
in the dark; let morning be broken only
by birdsong. Let us keep going, hand in hand....

Even So

Blessed be even this.
—Lucille Clifton

Even America First, though we weren't
the first, pushing the tribes ever westward.
Even though this country was built
with the labor of slaves, their blood soaked
into the red clay South. Even a senate so mean
they'd deny health care to the poor, the aged,
the disabled, to give the rich more tax breaks.
Blessed be. We have so much: oceans of fish,
fields of corn, herds of cattle. Who says
it's a pie, and if I get a slice, there's none
for you? Blessed be these sweet days
in October, the earth alchemized to gold.
Blessed be the undocumented, who pick
the grapes and bathe the dying. Blessed be
the single mother, working two jobs.
Blessed be the rich, the powerful, the entitled.
Someday, their hearts will crack open,
and they will see there are no borders.
Meanwhile, in a shining meadow
of goldenrod and asters, the bees
are humming, little captains of industry,
following the lure of pollen and the hot buzz
of hunger, to seal in wax hexagonals
a bit of sweetness, their IRAs and savings
accounts for the long nights of zero to come.

Sonnet from the Ephesians

—Ephesians 1:16

I do not cease to give thanks, especially in November
even as we lose an hour of light, drawing
the curtains at 4:30 to keep out the cold. To remember
you are dust seems appropriate now. Crows are cawing

black elegies in the bare trees. Just past the Day of the Dead,
and I'm thankful for every friend who has blessed
my life, gold coins in a wooden chest. Who said
no man is an island? We're all peninsulas, I guess,

joined to the mainland, part of the shore. We're the sticks
in the bundle that can't be broken. Even if
it doesn't seem that way, the bickering of politics,
the blather on the nightly news. Maybe we speak in hieroglyphs,
unclear, always missing the mark? So let me be plain.
I'm grateful for the days of sun. I'm grateful for the rain.

Today the River

Today, the *brouillard*, a wispy drape of muslin,
covers the Garonne. Thin, insubstantial, it won't last,
will burn off under the hot lamp of the October sun.
Unlike the solid stones of Chapelle Sainte-Catherine du Port,
patron saint of river workers, boatmen and sailors. And I've sailed
out of my everyday life to live by the river in an old mill,
near this chapel from Carolingian times. Mine's such a new country,
nothing in our history stretches back this far. So much to learn
from history's long reach. When they tried to torture Catherine
by tying her to a wheel, she shattered it with a touch. Mist rises
from the past, stones on which this chapel lies. Frescoes
from the 18th century peel and flake, but we can still see:
ships plying the river. Sails. A stained glass anchor.
Models of boats given in thanksgiving for safe journeys.
Sainte Catherine, I'm traversing this life without a compass
or sextant, and the current is treacherous. Burn off
the fog of doubt and uncertainty. Steer me through
these rapids, these shallows. Bring me safely into harbor.

American Robin

Here's that bird again, launching from the rhododendron,
banging his forehead on my living room window. *Thump.*
Thump. Does he see his own reflection in the glass
or does he see a rival, a threat to his nest? I hang
a black raptor silhouette in the middle square,
but that does not deter him. *Knock yourself out,*
I keep thinking. Next, I try cardboard, then a sheet
of newspaper smeared with its terrible
news. He comes back. Do I admire
him for his persistence or shrug
at his stupidity? *Thunk. Thunk.*

Today I read how fast the glaciers
are melting, the seas are rising, the Amazon
is on fire. We know what needs to be done,
but won't do it, and no amount of warning
seems to make us change our course. Up ahead:
the hard reckoning, the implacable glass pane.

Sonnet from Ecclesiastes

—Ecclesiastes 1:9

There's nothing new under the sun,
says the prophet, the leaves turning
brilliant colors right on time, one
of the things I love about the fall, this burning
without fire. Unbroken blue skies, home
of harvest, of plenty, combine blades churning
out rivers of golden corn. Our sojourn
on this earth, so brief. But I cannot play dumb,
storms are more violent, thousand-year floods
more frequent, and this government turns
a blind eye to misery and need. How can we let
it all slip through our fingers? Whiplashed by the moods
of politicians, their fistfuls of cash. Winter will return.
Will we see another spring? I will not be silent.

Forecast

Writing on a legal pad, extra-fine rollerball pen,
hoping for a poem, one that might, twenty-five drafts
later, appear in a magazine, or a "dead tree journal,"
as the kids might say. I recently read that no one
is reading anymore; attention spans shortened
to 140-character bursts. Goodbye Dickens. Farewell
Dostoevsky. The ice caps are melting,
and the forecast is: Extreme. Wine makes this
less extreme for an hour or so, but then the news comes on,
and all of it is bad. An administration so morally
bankrupt, comparing it to the Third Reich seems
like a foregone conclusion. Our government is constructing
camps, paying for this with our taxes. Contractors
fatten like ticks. At night, the sullen moon rises,
the air thick with humidity and insider trading.

We toss and turn, but the blood sun sears through the ozone,
while California burns. A little something sinister brewing
in the Gulf. And because no one is going to read this,
because I might as well chisel a stele
or scratch on papyrus, I yammer on.
Outside my window, a black and white woodpecker
is tapping, tapping his manifestos on a Royal typewriter.
The newspaper, with its terrible stories, rolls off the presses,
inky and black.

Messenger

after a poem with the same title by Mary Oliver

If, as Mary Oliver says, *my job is loving the world,*
then today it is easy: a bright sun, low humidity,
thin clouds frilling the sky. In the garden,
tomatoes are slowly fattening, eggplants
are sunning their purple rumps, and melons swell,
fat with juice. Everything in the process
of becoming. At the sugar feeder, hummingbirds
dart and whir in a busy blur, and the perennials
are going at it for all they're worth: blue-green
Russian sage, a river of golden daylilies,
white ruffled phlox, magenta loosestrife.
At dusk, swallows slice the air before the bats
come out. With all of this, why are we anxious?
Why is it difficult to share? Sweetness gathers.
It's summer, full to the brim. But out there,
brassy politicians trumpet: nuclear brinkmanship.
Drought and famine. Cities reduced to stones.
The rising seas. How can we balance
scarcity and surplus, greed and gratitude?
Why aren't we amazed by everything we have?

IV

Black and Purple Petunias #1

—*Georgia O'Keeffe*

Walking down the rows
of my local farm stand,
I think of the faith of the gardener,
who stuck something infinitesimal
in the ground, waited for the emergence
of the first pale leaves,
then the recognizable form.
Who pricked them into peat pots,
transplanted them in flats,
hauled them to this nursery,
where, needing some beauty in my life,
I brought them home,
tucked them in my perennial border.
Which is not guarded by a wall
or men with guns. Instead,
it pours its extravagant perfume,
its color, for the passers-by,
the joggers, the neighbors walking dogs.
I sit in the garden at twilight,
when the colors start shifting;
the dark ones, like these petunias,
receding; the light ones, like phlox,
coming into the foreground.
It's the equinox, darkness
and light in equal measure.
And here I am, trying
to keep my ears open
to every body's song.

Black and Purple Petunias #3

—Georgia O'Keeffe

She sat at my table, hands restless,
fiddling with the cracked teacup.
She flicked at her hair, twisted it
up with a clip, then let it loose,
falling over her collar, the white
blouse hiding the marks where
he gripped her, tight. She knew
they would bloom, black
and purple, a handful of night.

Poem Ending with a Line by Matisse

—Still Life with Geranium, by Henri Matisse

The heart of this painting is a width of Toile de Jouy,
cobalt curves and flowers on a pale blue wash.
More blue: the flat boards of the studio wall,
backdrop of this domestic drama, the cascading
cloth, the repeating patterns. From a simple clay pot,
a sunny geranium's red and pink flowers
commence their dance. *There are always flowers*
for those who want to see them, said Matisse.
I want to reach into the frame and crush
these green leaves, smell their acrid scent,
bury my face in the scarlet petals. *You have*
first of all to feel this light to find it in yourself.

Still Life with Dahlias

—Henri Matisse

This painting, in tones of French blue, is the *calme*
in *luxe, calme, et volupté*. It's also a page in my calendar
for the month of April, 1994, when my dog was still alive—
a red heart on the fourth reminded me to worm him—
where a note told me that my friend Harry, who has
now slipped into dementia, wanted to borrow some cross-
country poles. Leukemia hadn't claimed my dentist yet—
I had a cleaning on the 18th. I can see when report cards
came home, where I'd marked the days of Early Dismissal.
In the painting, the hot pink dahlias lined in Prussian blue
seem no more alive than the lighter pink roses
on the wallpaper or the peaches blushing on the plate.
Time has stopped in two dimensions: on the canvas
and in the calendar squares. The text, in the open
book on the cherry wood table, emits a faint blue
light. *Bonjour tristesse.* Is anything sadder than the past,
with its ruled notebooks, long-gone friends? Me,
when I didn't know the future? And yet the half-full
glass of water, cold from an old well, shimmers
with life. I know that when I raise it to my lips
it will give me some of what I've been longing for.

Late Painters: Matisse

Papier-découpé: form filtered to its essentials
—Henri Matisse

When his hands could no longer hold a brush,
Matisse turned to paper and scissors, "painting"
with cold metal carving heavy gouache
shearing shallow reliefs. The liberation of shape
from paper. And my left hand, too, betrays me,
mysteriously cramping, twisting like a snail in a shell.
No relief but to pry my fingers back into an ordinary
hand. And so the dance goes on. Confined to chair
or bed, Matisse's "seconde vie" lasted fourteen years,
as he learned to use white as a negative space,
working paper like a sculptor cutting through stone.
This is where I'd like to be working, reducing
the buzzing complicated world to its pure essence,
ridding myself of arabesques and complexities,
condensing the dance of my life in simple forms.

Une Seconde Vie

My curves are not crazy.
—Henri Matisse

In those last fourteen years, his eyesight failed,
and he was trapped in a wheelchair after a botched
operation for cancer. So he quit painting, reinvented
his art in cut-outs using tailors' scissors instead
of pen and ink or sable brushes. Since he could no longer
walk outside, he formed gardens from painted paper: fruit
flowers foliage. They bloomed where they were pinned,
to the flat white ground. Because he could no longer swim,
he said *I will make myself my own pool:* four walls
with wide panels of bright blue bodies diving, swimming,
floating on their backs, joyous as dolphins leaping
out of the sea. A draftsman to the end, he wielded
those two silver blades like a wild beast devouring its prey,
gnawing paper into forms. He caressed each contour
with hard metal, soft as a lover's touch. He saved both
the shapes and the scraps, secure in his use of negative space.
*I have needed all that time to reach the stage where I can say
what I want to say.* I am climbing that last hill as well; I hope
I will be able to murmur those words when the darkness thickens.

Late Painting: *Path Under the Rose Arches*

Monet is only an eye—yet what an eye.
—Paul Cézanne

A child's scribbles become the flowering arches,
broad scrawls, sprawls of color you can't quite see:
braided ribbons of burgundy, navy, sienna, ochre, umber.
Each arch opens a passage, a tunnel, a path that leads on.
No more working *en plein air*, no more striving for the elusive
moment. No more series: stacks of wheat, a cathedral
in sunlight, trains at the station; no more smoke, fog,
the sun lying down on the sheaves. So many ways
to say good-bye. The short, flicked brush strokes
that tried to catalog light's changes now become gestures,
swoops and swirls. Monet said *My poor eyesight makes
me see everything in a complete fog,* and I'm feeling this, too—
something not yet diagnosed, needing more light to read.

Typos flit on the screen, escape my scrutiny. Lines fly off
the page during a reading. But I'm not ready to quit,
and neither was he. Despite his growing cataracts,
he picked up a brush, having memorized the placement
of pigments on his palette, and started in on the water lilies,
les Grandes Décorations, from the garden of his memory,
removing the horizon, letting the flowers float
on a deep blue waterfall of radiant light.

Cathédrale Notre-Dame de Paris

April 15, 2019

Thus it is said:
The path into the light seems dark ...
—*Tao Te Ching*

Linked with the rest of the world as we are
via satellite and internet, I watched in horror
as the roof of Notre Dame and its filigreed spire
went up in flames. Nearly fifty years ago,
in the wreckage of my first marriage, I lit
a tall white taper, prayed that my husband
would return to himself, keep our family intact,
a prayer that disappeared in the dark vaults,
the deep shadows. Twenty years later, I returned,
recklessly in love with Paris and my new husband
in equal measure. We climbed to the roof, 387
stone steps, where the city spread out before us,
Hemingway's moveable feast. We kissed
each other hard, up there with the crouching
chimeras, strixes, the gargoyle waterspouts,
the flying buttresses, thinking that this time,
maybe we got it right, that this marriage
was built on solid rock, would last, forgetting
that nothing lasts, not the bronze bells, not
the glitter of the rose windows, not our little
lives, getting closer to the end. But even though
we know that restoration will take more than
our lifetime, and that we will not climb those
stairs again, in the vault of our memories
we are kissing. We are kissing as though
our lives depend on it; we are holding
each other tightly; we will never let go.

In Rome,

at the Palazzo Massimo, we saw the frescoed walls
   from the painted garden of the Villa of Livia, two thousand
years old, all hazy blues and greens. This is Eden, paradise regained.
   These walls were part of Livia's *triclinium*, a dining room partially
underground, cool in even the hottest summer months. Guests
   saw a garden of the imagination, so no beads
of perspiration decorated their brows. On these walls,
   all the blossoms bloom at once, and trees bear both flowers
and fruit, a natural impossibility: dates and quinces, myrtle
   and laurel, palm trees and oaks. While birds fly in the gentle
painted breeze: partridges, doves, and goldfinches, eating fruit,
   perching on limbs. Our limbs are weary, having tromped through
the Galleria Borghese, the Spanish Steps, the house where Keats
   gave his body to the skies, then the Trevi Fountain,
the Piazza Navona, and the Pantheon the day before, with the eye
   of the old gods shining down. I would like to settle, stay here,
recline on one of the imaginary couches, with peeled grapes,
   nightingale tongues, a fizzy drink embellished with pomegranate
seeds one of the birds has cut open. If I place them under
   my tongue, perhaps I can remain, basking in the sunshine
of this perpetual spring, and never grow old.

I Was Asked, What Did You Do in Rome?

Walked, with my bad knees, down the Spanish steps
to Bernini's stone bathtub, endlessly leaking.
John Keats died nearby unnoticed in a small room.

Stared at the Berninis at the Borghese, how he worked cold marble
as if it were dough—the indentation of Pluto's rough fingers
on Proserpina's thigh; Daphne's foot sprouting roots and leaves.

Ate gelato in all the colors of the *arcobaleno,*
the flavors of the tongue's longing: *cioccolato caffè,*
pistacchio, arancia, lavanda, limone, fragola, mirtillo.

Saw umbrella pines on the Appian Way.
Dark green cypresses pointing to the sky.
Beauty & graffiti, monuments & litter, fountains & ruins.

Stood open-mouthed in the Pantheon
at the oculus: blue sky mottled with clouds, light
floating down for two thousand years, the Eye of God.

Firenze

October, walking along the Arno, glazed in the saffron light
of late afternoon . . . Earlier, we'd been to the Accademia,
seen David—*Stop looking. I know you're looking*—said
the lecturer—the dimples on his knees, his magnificent *culo*.
What would it be like to spend just one night with that perfect man?
Today, the imperfections of our aging bodies become more evident:
my grinding knees, your screaming plantar fasciitis, which sent
you back to our hotel in a cab while I toured the Uffizi alone.
But oh, *La Primavera!* I want to be Flora, clothed in flowers:
forget-me-nots, daisies, buttercups, poppies, carnations, wild roses
circling my waist. But instead, I'm an aging woman in sensible shoes,
walking along the river alone, the light turning shifting shades
of tea-rose, lilac, peach, light that might be the lacquer
of an old master. I am trying not to stumble on the uneven pavement,
trying not to bump into impossibly chic women coming out of Gucci
and Prada carrying designer bags. The Ponte Vecchio looks tempting,
but we have dinner reservations near our hotel, where we will
hobble three blocks on the cobblestones, then eat *crostini, bistecca
alla fiorentina, Chianti, fragole con merina.* Age may have painted
us into a corner, tempered our desires, but when we finally lie down
at night, laying down the burdens of tendons and knees, we'll pull up,
not the high thread count sheets of this fine hotel, but the waters
of the Arno at sunset, colors of Prosecco, Bellinis, and let them
carry us off into the arms of night's soft chiaroscuro—

Annunciation

for my grandmother, Annunciata Cuccaro Poti

In Botticelli's *Cestello Annunciation*, the angel,
in a dusty rose robe, seems to have dropped
from the sky, overly eager to give the good news.
Which is not, it seems to me, how Mary receives
it, as she falls to her knees and twists toward the edge
of the frame. Wouldn't she feel framed herself
by these circumstances, unmarried and pregnant?
What is she going to tell her boyfriend? Who
would believe this incredible story? Look
at the tension between their hands, his reaching out,
hers pushing away. And yes, it's a miracle, God
come to Earth, the holy child, but who screams
in labor, whose world is split in two? Who pays
for this in milk and blood? Who had no choice,
but carried on, as women do?

Were We in Venice, or Was It a Dream?

Did we see palazzos, villas, churches floating
on their own dreamy reflections, the material world
rendered immaterial? Bridges, domes, spires, roofs,
all illusory? No land, just water. Thomas Mann
called it *half-fairy tale, half-tourist trap*. Did we really ride
on water: vaporetti, *gondole, traghetti*? Eat squid
in its own ink, *seppie al nero*, and polenta, listen
to Vivaldi in an old church, stop to see the moon
rise over the Accademia Bridge? Eat two gelatos a day?
Take a boat in the laguna, flat rippleless dreamscape,
to an *isola* where they pulled molten glass like taffy,
swirling it into petals, garlands, *millefiori*? Or visit
Burano, fishermen's cottages painted in an *arcobaleno*
pazzo: garish red, bilious green, screaming yellow,
electric blue the sky would be embarrassed to wear?
Nothing solid, not buildings but the doubles of buildings
shimmering on the canals. Each night on our hotel *terrazza*,
we had a Spritz, Aperol or Campari, garnished
with orange chunks, pineapple slices, cherries;
a libation and a daily fruit allowance all in one glass.
The sky is rubbed smooth, smudged with the pinks
and blues of an abstract pastel. I am wearing hand-blown
black earrings spangled with gold, the night sky in each ear.

Il Pranzo

We arrive masked, but not for a ball,
a careful six feet apart. Our hostess
has prepared lunch as if we were children
at a birthday party: our names on plastic cups,
napkins, disposable tableware all in a sealed
baggie. She brings out chips, wraps, fruit,
previously packaged, and pours our drinks:
Aperol spritzes, equal parts prosecco and bitter
aperitivo, sunset in a tumbler. And suddenly,
we are no longer in Pennsylvania looking
at a field of waving soybeans, but on a *terrazza*
in Venice on the Canal Grande, where our drinks
come with a garnish of fruit so spectacular,
it could be a Carnevale float. The water is turning
peach, aqua, citrus, the colors of Murano glass,
as the sun slowly sets. Nearby, night is waiting
to shrug into a dark velvet dress, don her mask
of sequins and stars.

Young Woman in Green, Outdoors in the Sun

—Mary Cassatt

Between the time her cataracts started to bloom—doctors
didn't treat civilians during the war—and when she renounced
painting altogether, she painted this girl in muted blues,
lush brushstrokes that characterized her later work.
The tone is somber, the hat bleeding into the shadows,
the looming trees. Cassatt's palette diminished,
shrunk to dark notes, just a glimpse of tropical yellows
and oranges in the sky.
                    Was she thinking about the war,
a sweetheart at the front? How hard it must have been
to be a woman then, twenty million dead, an equal number
wounded, and then the flu, what we're facing now,
this virus spreading, sped on its way by global traffic,
mass transit, our over-crowded world.
                    My cataracts are tiny buds, not large
enough to be harvested, but they prevent my driving at night,
create haloes when I come in out of the sun. I would like to be
as self-contained as the woman in this painting, hopeful,
yet resolute, with a splash of sunlight against the dark,
the brim of my hat a steady corona of light.

All My Poems Lately Are Elegies

Good-bye to old and dear friends who are slipping away;
adieu to clean air and water (thanks, deregulation);
sayonara to our wetlands that once sheltered us from storms;
ciao, arrivederci to our democracy and free press—what a lovely
experiment it was. Australia is on fire, and there's a nasty
virus coming out of China, fifty million in quarantine and rising.
The nightly news reports resemble opening scenes from a bad disaster
movie. This morning, low overcast sky, and suddenly, it's full
of snow geese, white from white, pouring out of a nearby quarry,
a river of wings. They, too, are saying good-bye.

My Only Time on the 6 PM News

for Darryl Dawkins, 1957-2015
NBA great

He was not only the nicest person I've ever met, he was also the best-looking corpse I've ever seen. He was in my Zumba class held three times a week in a fire hall. This giant of a man standing head and shoulders above our group of middle-aged women. Stevie Wonder gave him his nickname: Chocolate Thunder. Some years ago, he took a box of Skittles to his tailor (he was so tall, his clothes had to be custom made), and asked for a suit in every color. They dressed him in the red one with all of his diamond and gold jewelry—stunning. We wore our gym clothes and went as a group, then went to a bar afterwards to tell Darryl stories. It was a sports bar, so the evening news came on all seven large screen TVs. We weren't the celebrities—Larry Holmes, Billy Cunningham, the current Seventy-Sixers—so no one took our names, and the TV camera crew showed us from behind (most of our shirts or pants said ZUMBA). That was my only time on the evening news, and it was only my butt.

Valar Morghulis

"All men must die."
for Anya Silver, 1969-2019

And now, *Game of Thrones* has returned,
that blood-drenched guilty pleasure; an odd love,
perhaps, for pacifist poets, but nonetheless,
here it is, and we're hooked,

caught in its soap opera plot, its legend
and myth, its fantastic dragons. And I'm
pissed; you wanted so badly to live,
at least till the end of the series. But

the White Walkers came eight months ago. I want
to shake my fist at the sky, but what would be the point?
You are not going to return, like these familiar
characters we thought were dead

but now learn have survived the long hiatus.
At least for a few more weeks. Last April,
the last time I saw you, your hair had returned,
a cap of shining brown, Audrey Hepburn

or Jean Seberg in *Saint Joan*. Your gold hoop
earrings, your Ruby Woo lipstick, which I am
now wearing in your memory, lit up your face.
We were iced in, Grand Rapids, Michigan, flight

after flight cancelled, texting like crazy.
Eventually, we all made it home. But we
had plans: a panel at a conference,
a manuscript to finish, new poems to write.

Are you beyond The Wall of ice, enjoying
the long summer, drinking Dornish wine?
Do you know the end of the story?
I know nothing,

like Jon Snow. Except that your poems
were on fire, beacons to guide us
through dark nights, full of terror.
And that they will not be extinguished.

A Villanelle for Kim

in memoriam Kim Bridgford, 1959-2020

If there was a poetry goddess, you were it:
teacher, writer, scholar, editor—
When things were tough, you didn't quit;

you stood your ground, did the opposite
of what the other side expected. Sure,
there's a poetry goddess, and you were it.

You rose above the fray: the bullshit,
faculty politics. How unfair then: cancer.
When things got tough, you wouldn't quit.

You showed us how to live, with grace and wit.
Keep going when it's hard, rise up, endure.
If there's a poetry goddess, you were it.

But now you're gone, I'm reading your obit.
This wasn't something medicine could cure.
Though things were rough, you didn't quit.

And so, our memories: sunlit.
No darkness. Salt air and lilacs, copper
beech leaves shining. Poetry goddess, you are it.
Things were tough. You never quit.

Ceremonies of Grief

And where you are is where you are not.
—*T. S. Eliot, "East Coker"*
for Clare Reidy

What was it that happened in the clearing,
the one you wrote about in your last poem?
Was there *a sudden clarity, a light,*

or did *a greater darkness prevail?*
You'd asked, *What will I become?*
Another question with no answer.

What will become of us, you didn't
ask, stranded here without you?
At your funeral Frank slid into

the pew next to me, then asked,
Are you ready? I thought he meant
for your death, but no, he wanted to know

if I'd bought my plot yet, that bed with
green sheets and hard white pillows.
I wanted to say *we're too young,*

but I know these will be the gatherings
we'll be going to now, not weddings
or baptisms. Today, I'm down

by the creek, a scatter of purple
violets rising from heart-shaped leaves.
The stream sings its nonsense

song, running from here to there, always
in a hurry, moving through the clearing.
Nothing stops it. It keeps going on.

Ohio Blue Tip

for Len

His father came back time after time as a chattering finch,
but I think my old friend's returned as a jay, the flashy
spots of white on wings and tail like the shock
of white his hair turned, young. He's a bold bird,
as our Emily said, writing about forbidden subjects—
blowjobs in back seats, Thorazine and electro-shock,
the nine names of God. He's feathered with the sky.
You can always spot jays by the beat of their wings,
their flight patterns, the way they keep on going. They're
common, everyday, in neighborhood yards and hedgerows.
But when they're gone, don't we miss them, those hot blue
flames, as if a cold draft had suddenly entered the room,
and blown out the pilot light, just like that.

Some Fine Day

also for Len

Yesterday, all the stars were in their proper places.
The earth was waiting to turn green, the peach
tree about to blossom, tint the air pink, bring
in the bees. One phone call, and everything
shifts, a longtime friend's suddenly terminal,
his body turning on his heart and lungs.
I don't want to open the door
to blossoming yard, the cotton candy air,
songs of newly returned birds.
I want to roll up the fake backdrop
of the hopeful blue sky, call back
the days of steady rain, let the coldness
linger. How can we go on, knowing the end
of the story? The lawn greens up anyway,
tossing out its thin curls of cellophane,
the lining for a basket of pastel eggs,
pink and blue and gold, we already know
are cracked.

Elegy on a Line by Merton

for Charles

Tuesday morning in the grove of the Jesuit novitiate,
and the sky is blue as Mary's robes in any painting
of the Renaissance. Everything slowly turning to gold;
the leaves that are ready, let go, fall on the lawn,
a brilliant crazy quilt. There's a turkey vulture
winging on the thermals, swinging low, and a train
rumbles slow in the east. We know the hairs on our heads
are numbered, but we can't believe our story will have
an ending. We think next year will be the same, the maples
turning sulphur yellow, dogwoods crimson, sumac
heart's blood. In the hospice, you're at the end
of your journey; the conductor has given your ticket
its final punch. There's an edge of brightness
around every leaf. *Everything that can be desired*
will sear you.

Cirque D'Hiver

The dead are seated in rows at the Cirque d'hiver;
they cannot remain quiet anymore, they want
to have something to cheer about, need to have
something to applaud. They have missed Cracker
Jacks, cotton candy, peanuts in paper sacks.
They love the clown with his greasepaint smile,
the little dogs in their ruffled collars, the magician
pulling silks from his sleeve. They don't need
the marquee acts, the motorcycle turning circles
in a cage, the woman dancing on a silver wire
high above the crowd, the tigers with their meaty
breath. The dead want sawdust, the smoke
that lingers after the cannon goes off, the steaming
pile the elephant leaves. Even that.

Blue Christmas

the name of a relatively new Advent service for mourners

This has been a dark year, when the arm of the angel of death
has grown sore from swinging his heavy scythe, eleven sharp
strokes in my circle of friends. And now it's December,
when the rest of the world glitters like sugar, when stores
drip tinsel and ribbons, and the air in the mall is thick
with carols. For those who mourn, the sky is the color
of soot, and white lights hung on pines do nothing
to dispel the gloom. The year burns down to ashes,
calendar pages go up in flakes of char, the reverse of birds.
Going to the store for milk and eggs before it snows
is a minefield; you are bound to bump into someone
you haven't seen in years who asks about your family—
Then there's the checkout girl with the reindeer hat
who brightly tells you to have a happy holiday,
and you can't reply. Sympathy cards are stuffed
in the mailbox's craw. If you can get dressed
before night falls down like a jail door clanging,
it's been a good day. In the houses of mourning,
the holidays weigh like a heavy sack.
In the corner, the empty chair.

VI

Credo

It's early summer, everything running to green,
and the sun has dipped its brush in gilt: coreopsis,
black-eyed Susans, Stella d'Oro lilies. At night,
the cool moon throws a silver net over
the darkened yard. You can till the earth,
hoe the rows, but each seed is an act of belief
that somehow in the dark something
is happening: seeds splitting their husks,
softened by rain and spray from the hose,
then sending up pale shoots, periscopes
searching for light. Two leaves, four leaves,
and suddenly: a vine. Which has a mind
of its own, trellising up the tomatoes,
smothering the beans. Remove the coils
used for a foothold, place it in the space
between rows, so it can grow longer, greener
every day. Nobody ever sees this happen;
we take it on faith. Next come little lemon stars,
then small green globes, which swell, fill,
fueled by the sun. The calendar turns to August,
days ripen, each one more golden than the next.
Nothing the gardener does can make this happen.
One morning, when the leaves are slick with dew,
you go out to check and realize every rib
is yellow, the netting is even, webbed with gold,
and that which has held fast throughout this long
season is ready to slip, fill your hands with its heft,
fill your bowl with roundness, and soon, nestled
in the boat of your spoon, the sun's longing
exploding on your tongue.

Plum

Thumbprint of the moon,
blush of the summer sky.
A rim of sweetness
hemmed in damask.
Bruise-blue, ruby red,
autumn gold; the full
spectrum of sugar.
The thrum of a tenor sax.
You brood on the tree,
biding your time.
If we're lucky, we'll
find you whole, oval,
unstung by wasps,
ungnawed by squirrels.
You will fill
a child's palm.
Hot juice
of an August night,
a gulp of dark wine.
A taste
that winter,
which we know
is coming,
cannot erase.

Late Night Martinis

Out beyond the ambient light, glass
of gin, rumor of vermouth, a few olives,
we're sitting on black wrought iron lawn chairs,
talking poetry & friendship, love & loss.
Above us, the indifferent stars glitter
cold light. A chorus of coyotes
calls from the woods. We're told
we come from spindrift and stardust.
No doubt about the dust to which we will
return. Those stars are set in their patterns:
there's a ladle, a dragon, a celestial belt.
We wobble in our orbits, unsure and alone.
Will there be a gathering by the river
or a blank nothing at the end of the day?
My long-stemmed glass, which is now
half-empty, seems to me half-full.

And Now It's September,

and the garden diminishes: cucumber leaves rumpled
and rusty, zucchini felled by borers, tomatoes sparse
on the vines. But out in the perennial beds, there's one last
blast of color: ignitions of goldenrod, flamboyant
asters, spiraling mums, all those flashy spikes waving
in the wind, conducting summer's final notes.
The ornamental grasses have gone to seed, haloed
in the last light. Nights grow chilly, but the days
are still warm; I wear the sun like a shawl on my neck
and arms. Hundreds of blackbirds ribbon in, settle
in the trees, so many black leaves, then, just as suddenly,
they're gone. This is autumn's great Departure Gate,
and everyone, boarding passes in hand, waits
patiently in a long, long line.

Today

Swing low, turkey vulture, rocking on your dihedral,
flake of char from the campfire of the blazing trees.
Someone has washed the sky and hung it up to dry,
just for you. In the meadow below, small insects
are ringing their discordant bells, autumn's last song.
A Monarch floats by with its stained-glass wings,
on its way to Mexico. *Adios, adios.* Go with God.
Beyond these blue hills, the rich and powerful
make deals, fatten their purses. As the gap widens,
misery increases. But this is copper October,
a bright uncloudy day. The sun pours gold coins
in everyone's pockets. Can you hear their jingle
when the wind blows through the leaves?

Lux Perpetua

and you, my friend, out there somewhere,
still ahead of us in the light.
—Christopher Buckley on Larry Levis
for Susan Elbe

A light that's glancing off the hickory leaves,
reflecting the October sun. The world dims,
the dousing of a flame in the hearth. There's copper
and bronze in the trees, goldenrod lighting the meadows;
squirrels are digging in, storing their hoard, and bees return
to the hive, summer's sweetness sealed in wax.
The sky is still heartache blue, but November
is coming, with its afghan of gray, threaded by geese,
everything gone to seed. Sitting by the fire
with a tumbler of whisky, I raise a glass to you,
old friend. So many words unsung: flocks of birds
gathering in stanzas on telephone wires, ready to lift
into the bright endlessness at a moment's startle.

Mid-November,

and the wind is having its way with the trees.
The cold air resonates with crows making
casual conversation, mocking remarks.
As the woods thin, the bones become visible,
and smoke from the chimneys braids hand over
hand, almost reaching the clouds. This is the pause
before the holidays' razzle-dazzle gives way to winter,
the year's interior. The sun sinks in the west, a teabag
in hot water; citrus and cinnamon fill the room.
Night comes quickly now, the click of a camera shutter.
From the copse on the edge of the meadow, a murmuration
of starlings, a river of birds, clamorous cacophony,
weaving and unweaving the air.

February

Snow-covered fields rolling out on either side,
like the gauze that covers my foot and ankle,
the wound that just won't heal. An abscess
like an absence, this blank landscape,
the black alphabet of trees. It's too cold
to be out; small animals huddle in burrows
or shelter in hedgerows. Too cold for most birds
to be flying. Already, the losses adding up:
my cousin's husband who didn't wake up;
two high school friends who walked down
that long corridor; the friend who suddenly
couldn't breathe in the middle of the night.
It's the season of no return, no coming back
with the green grass and crocuses
doing their hocus-pocus with purple and gold
scarves. No, this is what isn't: the unreturned
phone call, the unanswered text, the unwritten email,
the empty chair. This is it, the last inning, the final
quarter, the must-be-met deadline. Every field,
every hollow, fills up with snow.

Good-bye, Winter, You Bad Boyfriend;

hit the gravel-strewn road. Take your cold shoulder with you,
your icy breath. I'm tired of your hard freezes, the little snow squalls
that litter the ground like so many flakes of dandruff. I want a new
man, with a soft touch, who brings me jonquils in green tissue paper,
whose voice is like rain, who paints the sky robin's egg blue,
just for me, just because I want it.

Ode to April

Nothing shy about you as you paint the sky
   with thick blue impasto, a gusto that's
echoed in the blare of daffodils, their horn
   section discordant in the wind. Which spins
the forsythia into a new way of dancing: jazz
   hands. Jazz hands. A brass band
in every shade of gold. Who was it who told us
   it couldn't stay? But now hooray! for the lilacs,
their purple credenzas, the stanzas of violets
   dotting the lawn. It's a procession, the progression
of one flower after another, serial lovers to pluck
   and discard. Winter was hard, the yard brown,
the garden bare. Along comes April,
   with her one sweet song. And then, without
missing a beat, here comes May, with her ruffled
   skirt, skimpy shirt, and columbines in her hair.

Forsythia

What must it feel like,
after months of existing
as bare brown sticks,
all reasonable hope
of blossoming lost,
to suddenly, one warm
April morning, burst
into wild yellow song,
hundreds of tiny prayer
flags rippling in the still-
cold wind, the only flash
of color in the dull yard,
these small scraps of light,
something we might
hold on to.

Happiness

Whoever can see through all fear
Will always be safe.
—Tao Te Ching

It's a day of brilliant blue, lightly smudged
with chalky clouds. In the larger world, there's
fracking, climate change, industrial sludge.
But here, none of this can reach us. Who cares

about the news? I'm in this lawn chair,
secure in its embrace. In the distance,

the surf of traffic, the hum of bees. Chances
are, none of us gets to live forever.
The shadow of the vulture on the lawn
cannot dispel this blue euphoria.

About the Author

Barbara Crooker is author of twelve chapbooks and nine full-length books of poetry. A recent collection, *Some Glad Morning*, Pitt Poetry Series, University of Pittsburgh Poetry Press, was longlisted for the Julie Suk award from Jacar Press. Her previous collection, *The Book of Kellls*, won the Best Poetry Book of 2019 Award from Poetry by the Sea. Her other awards include: Grammy Spoken Word Finalist, the WB Yeats Society of New York Award, the Thomas Merton Poetry of the Sacred Award, and three Pennsylvania Council fellowships in literature. Her work appears in literary journals and anthologies, including *The Bedford Introduction to Literature*.

Acknowledgments

823 on High: "Cirque d'Hiver"

Ars Medica: "Acupuncture"

Blueline: "Elegy on a Line by Merton" (published as "Elegy")

Comstock Review: "Today," "Lux Perpetua"

Connecticut River Review: "Mid-November"

Constellation: "Late Painters: Matisse"

Gargoyle: "Black and Purple Petunias #3"

here: "Black and Purple Petunias #1"

Hollins Critic: "Ohio Blue Tip"

I-70 Review: "Queens," "Mussels," *"Young Woman in Green"*

JAMA: "Degenerative Disc Disorder"

Juniper: "Good-Bye, Winter, You Bad Boyfriend;"

Life & Legends: "Ceremonies of Grief"

Light: "Treadmill"

Live Encounters: "On a Late Birthday" (published as "At Seventy"), "And It's Hard," "Love in These Dangerous Times," "In Rome," "Ode to April"

Mezzo Cammin: "Obsolescence," "Weight Training"

Michigan Quarterly Review: "Mirror"

Mom Egg Review: "Pentimento"

New World: "Who Do You Carry?"

Nimrod: "After Rotator Cuff Surgery"

One: "Poem Ending with a Line by Matisse" (published as *"Still Life with Geranium"*), "Firenze"

Perspectives: "Blue Christmas"

Pittsburgh Quarterly: "Some Fine Day"

Plant-Human Quarterly: "Credo"

Poems for Ephesians: "Sonnet from the Ephesians"

Poet Lore: "U Pick"

Presence: "A Villanelle for Kim"

Quiddity: "Happiness"

Relief: "Sonnet from Ecclesiastes," "Annunciation"

Salt: "Car Hop," "Cathédrale Notre-Dame de Paris," "All My Poems Lately Are Elegies," "My Only Time on the 6 PM News"

Spillway: "And Now It's September"

Talking River Review: "I Was Asked, What Did You Do in Rome?" "Une Seconde Vie"

The Gathering: "Forsythia"

The Healing Muse: "After Oral Surgery"

The Innisfree Poetry Journal: "Messenger," "February"

The MacGuffin: "Then," "Credo," "Seventieth Birthday"

The Paterson Literary Review: "On Teaching Poetry Classes in My Old Elementary School," "Aphorisms at Seventy," "American Robin," "Were We in Venice, or Was It a Dream?," "Valar Morghulis"

The Valparaiso Poetry Review: "Diorama," "Late Painting: *Path Under the Rose Arches*"

Upstreet: "*Still Life with Dahlias*"

US One Worksheets: "Plum"

Whale Road Review: "American Plane Tree," "I Want to Write a Poem to Celebrate"

Windhover: "Today the River"

"I Want to Write a Poem to Celebrate," "Treadmill," "Credo" "Il Pranzo," "Mussels," and "Young Woman in Green" were nominated for the Pushcart Prize. "And Now It's September" also appeared in *An American Life in Poetry*. "Forsythia" also appeared in *More in Time: A Ted Kooser Tribute* (University of Nebraska Press) and *The Path to Kindness* (Storey Publishing). "U Pick," "After Oral Surgery," and "Credo" also appeared in *Food, Glorious Food* (Kraziness). "U Pick" and "Queens" also appeared in *Poetry of Presence: An Anthology of Mindfulness Poems, Vol. 2* (Grayson Books).

Many thanks to The Virginia Center for the Creative Arts for the time and space in which to write these poems, to Marjorie Stelmach for her keen editorial eyes and ears, to Christopher Buckley for his excellent suggestions, and to Mike Mirarchi, proofreader extraordinaire.